BISON

Curious Kids Press

Bison

The bison is not a buffalo (as many people assume). Millions of bison once roamed the North American plains. Today, the numbers have fallen due to hunting and habitat loss. The bison played a major role in the lives of the natives of this area. It was used as food and to make clothing from. There is so much more to learn about the bison, so let's get started and explore the fascinating world of this huge animal.

Where in the World?

Did you know the American bison almost became extinct? These mighty beasts were found all over North America, but are now only located in small populations. National parks like Yellowstone and Wood Buffalo, keep small herds of these animals safe and protected. Bison live on flat open land and on prairies.

The Body of a Bison

Did you know the bison can stand over 6 feet tall and that is just to its shoulder? Bison are large, burly beasts. It can measure from 10 to 12.5 feet long and weigh from 900 to 2,000 pounds. It also has a large head and a big hump on its upper back.

The Bison's Fur

Did you know the bison has thick shaggy fur around its head and neck? This thick fur also extends down to its front legs. However, the back and hind end of the bison only has short hair. The bison also sports a long thick beard. The coat of this animal is so thick, that snow doesn't even melt on it.

The Bison's Horns

Did you know the bison grows horns? Both the male and female bison will grow horns. This starts around 4 years of age. The older the bison gets, the longer its horns will grow. The horns play an important role in the bison's life. They are used to defend itself with. In fact, the bison will rub its horns on trees to sharpen them.

The Wallowing Bison

Did you know the bison rolls on the ground to stay clean? In the summer months, the bison is bothered by insects. These nasty pests bite and lay eggs on the bison. So to help stop this, the bison will wallow (roll) on the ground. This scraps off the insects and their eggs, as well as any old fur.

What a Bison Eats

Did you know the bison spends most of its time eating? This animal likes to eat grass, wild oats, rye, wheat, lichens, grass-like weeds and berries. The bison starts to graze (or eat) in the early morning. Like a cow, it will swallow lots of food, then bring it back up and chew it. This is called, cud.

The Bison's Senses

Did you know it is hard to sneak up on a bison? This animal has an excellent sense of hearing and smell. This alerts it to predators. Its wide flat nose can pick up the scent of a predator from a great distance away. However, the bison does have small eyes and poor eyesight.

The Bison's Special Ability

Did you know although the bison is very strong alone, as a group they are even more powerful? When a herd of bison are frightened they will all run together. This is called a stampede and you better move out of the way. These charging animals will flattened anything in their path.

The Bison as Prey

Did you know even though the bison is very large it still have predators? Animals such as the grizzly bear, mountain lion, wolves and coyotes all hunt the bison. Since the bison is so big, it is usually just the very young, weak or injured bison that are preyed upon. Man also hunts the bison for its meat and pelt.

Bison Talk

Did you know the bison can communicate? The bison can grunt, snort and growl. These sounds are usually made when this animal is irritated or angry. Most of the bison's communication is done through the sense of smell. Female bison give off a special pheromone (smell) that tells the male bison she is ready to have young.

Mother Bison

Did you know the female bison is called a cow? The cow is ready to breed between the ages of 2 and 3. She will carry her baby throughout the fall and winter and into the early spring. She will give birth to one baby and care for it for several months.

Baby Bison

Did you know the baby bison is called a calf? The baby bison is born already weighing 50 pounds and it has reddish-colored fur. Within the first hour of its birth, it can already stand up. Soon after this it will learn to walk. The calf will nurse milk from its mother.

Life of a Bison

Did you know bison migrate in the winter months? Wild bison will move to places where the food is more plentiful in the winter months. Sometimes this requires them to travel for hundreds of miles. Once a bison makes it to adulthood, it can live from 20 to 25 years of age.

Wood Bison

This type of bison is a cousin to the American bison. The wood bison is the largest of them all. It can weigh upwards of 1,600 pounds and may live to be 40 years-old! It is found in Northern Canada. It has a super-large head and can run up to 35 miles-per-hour.

Quiz

Question 1: What other animal is the bison often mistaken for?

Answer 1: A buffalo

Question 2: What odd feature does the bison have?

Answer 2: It has a big hump on its back

Question 3: What does the bison have in common with a cow?

Answer 3: They both chew their cuds

Question 4: When a group of bison all run together, what is this called?

Answer 4: A stampede

Question 5: Newborn buffalos are very large. How much do they weigh?

Answer 5: Around 50 pounds

Thank you for checking out another addition from Curious Kids Press! Make sure to check out Amazon.com for many other great titles.